THE EXTRAORDINARY LIFE OF
NELSON
MANDELA

First American Edition 2020
Kane Miller, A Division of EDC Publishing

Original edition first published by Penguin Books Ltd, London
Text copyright © E.L. Norry 2020
Illustrations copyright © Ashley Evans 2020
The author and the illustrator have asserted their moral rights.

For information contact:
Kane Miller, A Division of EDC Publishing
P.O. Box 470663
Tulsa, OK 74147-0663
www.kanemiller.com
www.usbornebooksandmore.com

Library of Congress Control Number: 2020937643

Printed and bound in the United States of America
1 2 3 4 5 6 7 8 9 10
ISBN: 978-1-68464-199-4

THE EXTRAORDINARY LIFE OF
NELSON
MANDELA

Written by E. L. Norry
Illustrated by Ashley Evans

Kane Miller
A DIVISION OF EDC PUBLISHING

South Africa

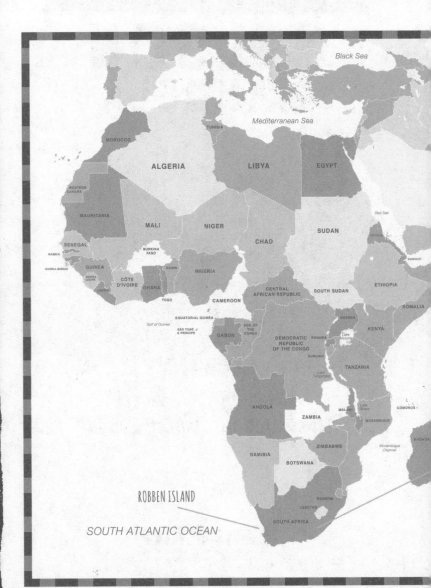

Black Sea

Mediterranean Sea

MOROCCO

TUNISIA

ALGERIA

LIBYA

EGYPT

WESTERN SAHARA

Red Sea

MAURITANIA

MALI

NIGER

SUDAN

SENEGAL

CHAD

GAMBIA

BURKINA FASO

GUINEA-BISSAU

GUINEA

BENIN

NIGERIA

DJIBOUTI

SIERRA LEONE

CÔTE D'IVOIRE

GHANA

TOGO

LIBERIA

CAMEROON

CENTRAL AFRICAN REPUBLIC

SOUTH SUDAN

ETHIOPIA

SOMALIA

Gulf of Guinea

EQUATORIAL GUINEA

SÃO TOMÉ & PRÍNCIPE

GABON

REP. OF THE CONGO

UGANDA

KENYA

DEMOCRATIC REPUBLIC OF THE CONGO

RWANDA

Lake Victoria

BURUNDI

TANZANIA

Lake Tanganyika

ANGOLA

MALAWI

Lake Nyasa

COMOROS

ZAMBIA

MOZAMBIQUE

MADAGASCAR

Mozambique Channel

ZIMBABWE

NAMIBIA

BOTSWANA

ROBBEN ISLAND

ESWATINI

LESOTHO

SOUTH AFRICA

SOUTH ATLANTIC OCEAN

Aral Sea
Gulf of Oman
ZIMBABWE
Bulawayo
NAMIBIA
Windhoek
Walvis Bay
BOTSWANA
Gaborone
Pretoria
Maputo
Johannesburg
Mbabane
ESWATINI
LESOTHO
Maseru
Durban
SOUTH AFRICA
Port Elizabeth
Cape Town
MAURITIUS

WHO WAS
Nelson
Mandela?

Nelson Mandela

was born on July 18, 1918, in the small village
of Mvezo, in the Transkei area of South Africa.
He grew up to be a lawyer and the leader of the ANC
(African National Congress) political party. Nelson
has become an inspiration to people all over the
world who strive for freedom and EQUALITY.

EQUALITY:
everyone has the same
rights and opportunities,
no matter where they
come from or what they
look like.

He fought against APARTHEID and for **equal rights** for black South Africans for more than fifty years.

APARTHEID:
in South Africa, the racist system of apartheid meant that people were separated because of the color of their skin.

Nelson Mandela believed that all people should be treated the same, no matter what color their skin. He was **arrested** several times by the government for breaking the law, and eventually, in 1964, he received a prison *life sentence*.

After twenty-seven years in prison, Nelson Mandela was finally set free. After a historic election in 1994, where South Africans of every ETHNIC BACKGROUND could vote for the first time ever, he became the *first black South African president*.

ETHNIC BACKGROUND:

a way of defining someone by the heritage they were born with; their parents and grandparents being considered members of specific national, racial, or religious groups. Skin color is one way many identify with a particular heritage.

"No one is born hating another person because of THE COLOR OF HIS SKIN, OR HIS BACKGROUND, OR HIS RELIGION.

People must learn to hate, and if they can learn to hate, THEY CAN BE TAUGHT TO LOVE, for love comes more naturally to the human heart than its opposite."

Let's find out more about Nelson and his extraordinary life.

Nelson's beginnings

*N*elson Mandela wasn't always called Nelson. When he was born in Mvezo, he was named Rolihlahla.

DID YOU KNOW?

Rolihlahla means "pulling the branch of a tree," though it is more commonly translated as "troublemaker."

Xhosa

The **Xhosa** people are an ethnic group from southern Africa. Nelson Mandela's people were Xhosa. The Xhosa nation is made up of different *tribes and clans*.

Tribes and clans

A group of people who share the same ancestry or culture can be called a *tribe*. Tribes usually live in their own enclosed society. The **Thembu** are one tribe of the Xhosa people, and Nelson was brought up in the traditions of the **Thembu** people.

Clans are groups of families. **Madiba** was the clan Nelson belonged to. All members of the clan could be called Madiba. Being called by your clan name was a sign of respect and affection.

"Each Xhosa belongs to a clan that traces its descent back to a specific forefather. I AM A MEMBER OF THE MADIBA CLAN, NAMED AFTER A THEMBU CHIEF who ruled in the Transkei in the eighteenth century."

The way the Thembu lived their lives in South Africa was different from how we might live today. *Traditions and beliefs* had been passed down to them from other Thembu for hundreds of years.

Nelson's father, Gadla Henry Mphakanyiswa, was the *chief* of a tribe and the village leader. He was an important man. When people couldn't agree about things, Gadla settled the village arguments. He gave advice and helped other Thembu chiefs.

He had four wives, and would travel around, spending time with each wife at different times. Nelson had many siblings – three sisters, three half brothers and six half sisters.

His mother, Nosekemi Nkedama, kept livestock and grew crops.

Mvezo was a small, quiet place, with many hills and open spaces around. Nelson was used to *freedom* and a simple life in the countryside. He played in the hills and swam in the nearby streams.

He also had chores to do to help his family. Nelson was a **herd boy** by age five, looking after the family's goats and sheep.

"*I learned how to*
KNOCK BIRDS OUT OF THE SKY
WITH A SLINGSHOT,
to gather wild honey

AND FRUITS AND EDIBLE ROOTS,
to drink warm, sweet milk
straight from the
udder of a cow . . ."

Racism in South Africa

Europeans in South Africa

The Xhosa and Zulus were two of the largest groups of people living in South Africa, which was made up of lots of different areas.

In 1652, Dutch settlers arrived in South Africa, forcibly taking land and fighting with the native South Africans. In 1806 the British arrived, interested in all the gold and diamonds in the areas where the Dutch had settled. This resulted in a long conflict: the Boer War. "Boer" is the Dutch word for "farmer."

Eventually the British won the Boer War and took control of South Africa. All the different areas became one country – the Union of South Africa – in 1910, as a territory of the British Empire, ruled by a white minority.

The white government treated black
South Africans unfairly. They made
laws that meant you could only
vote if you owned property, which
many black people didn't.

Changes for Nelson's family

*O*ne day, Nelson's father was supposed to attend a meeting at his job to discuss a complaint someone had made about cattle. But, he was a very *proud* man, and he did not go to the meeting because he believed it was beneath him. Unfortunately, the man in charge fired him. This was bad news. Suddenly, there was no money coming in to provide for the family.

The family needed to leave Mvezo. Nelson's mother took him and his sisters to live with some aunts and cousins in a bigger nearby village called *Qunu* – she knew they would be looked after there. Nelson's father *visited* them often.

"Huts were beehive-shaped structures of mud walls, WITH A WOODEN POLE IN THE CENTER HOLDING UP A PEAKED GRASS ROOF."

In Qunu, Nelson only met a few white people – the local shopkeeper and magistrate.

Many children couldn't read or write, and most didn't go to school. They learned customs and beliefs from their elders, and helped their families with the livestock and crops.

Friends of Nelson's father, however, saw Nelson playing and noticed he was clever. They suggested to Nelson's mother that he should be sent to *school*. She agreed, making Nelson the first in his family to attend school. This was a big deal! He was seven years old.

"EDUCATION IS THE
GREAT ENGINE OF PERSONAL
DEVELOPMENT.

*It is through education
that the daughter of a peasant
can become*

A DOCTOR,

*that the son of a mine worker
can become*

THE HEAD OF THAT MINE,

*that a child of farmworkers
can become*

THE PRESIDENT OF
A GREAT NATION."

For his first day of school, Nelson wore a pair of his dad's trousers, cut off so they'd fit him.

Once he was at elementary school, the English name of "Nelson" was given to him by his teacher Miss Mdingane.

White people didn't like to use tribal names that they could not pronounce, so often teachers gave the children English-sounding names. These were often the names of famous people from white history. Do you think this was fair?

"Why she bestowed this particular name on me I have no idea. Perhaps it had something to do with

THE GREAT BRITISH SEA CAPTAIN LORD NELSON,

but that would be only a guess."

When Nelson was nine, his father, Gadla, passed away from a lung disease. Nelson's mother decided that the family now needed to leave Qunu to travel to Mqhekezweni. In their tribe, learning from the *elders* how to be a man was important for every boy, and she wanted Nelson to grow up with a *male role model*. The king of the Thembu, *Chief Jongintaba*, had been friends with Nelson's father. He had promised that he would look after Nelson himself, if Gadla died.

Nelson and his mother walked for more than a whole day to reach Mqhekezweni, the Great Place, which is where Chief Jongintaba lived.

Mqhekezweni was more WESTERNIZED than anywhere Nelson had lived before. He saw houses and huts bigger than he'd ever seen! His world was opening up.

WESTERNIZED:
inspired by European and American cultures.

"In that moment of beholding Jongintaba and his court . . .

I FELT A SENSE OF AWE

mixed with

BEWILDERMENT."

Life at the Great Place

Chief Jongintaba and his wife had their own children, a son called *Justice* (four years older than Nelson) and a daughter called *Nomafu*.

Nelson was welcomed into their family and lived happily with them for many years.

This lifestyle was very different from what Nelson had been used to. Here, people dressed in *modern* clothes, while Nelson had been used to often wearing just a blanket tied at the shoulder.

DID YOU KNOW?

Cars weren't common in those days, and Nelson saw his first car when he saw the chief driving an old Ford V8.

Nelson went to church, helped iron the chief's suits, and herded sheep, but he also had fun by riding horses, playing with slingshots, stick fighting, and singing Xhosa songs.

At tribal meetings, Nelson saw the way the chief listened to and helped his people by settling arguments and advising people. Nelson learned about *being fair* and patient and kind. From other leaders, Nelson heard stories about African culture and history, and heard what life had been like for the black South Africans before the Europeans had arrived.

Nelson's education

The chief wanted Nelson to have a good education and to follow in his father's footsteps by becoming an ADVISER. He sent him to the *Clarkebury Institute* – a Methodist high school more than fifty miles away. Here, from the age of sixteen, Nelson had lessons in English, history, geography, and Xhosa.

ADVISER: one who helps others to sort out their disagreements. An important role in the community.

Nelson's previous school had only consisted of one room, but Clarkebury had more than twenty different buildings. It was here at Clarkebury that Nelson shook hands with a white man for the first time: the principal, Reverend Harris.

All the pupils did physical work along with their studies. Nelson worked in the reverend's garden.

At age nineteen, Nelson then attended *Healdtown College* for two years. Nelson had a strict routine there. He enjoyed sports where DISCIPLINE is important, like long-distance running and boxing. Little did he know it, but these personal skills, as well as his love of gardening, would come in useful when he later spent a long time in prison.

DISCIPLINE:
using self-control to train and improve your body and/or mind.

Fort Hare University

Nelson was twenty-one when he went to a bigger university called *Fort Hare*. He met Oliver Tambo here, and they went on to become good friends. Nelson also learned ballroom dancing and was in a play about Abraham Lincoln.

DID YOU KNOW?

Nelson received a brand-new pair of boots from Chief Jongintaba as a present for starting at the university.

At this time, Nelson wanted to become a CIVIL SERVANT. Being at a bigger university meant that Nelson met many different types of people.

CIVIL SERVANT: person who works for the government.

Nelson was elected to the **student representative council**. He was asked by some students to help them get better food. Nelson wanted to help, but he decided to resign from the council because a student BOYCOTT about the food served meant that only a few students had voted for the student representatives. He believed he shouldn't represent the students unless *everyone* had voted, so that it was fair.

BOYCOTT: a protest that means you stop buying from, or dealing with, a certain organization or country.

The headmaster threatened to *expel* Nelson if he resigned, but when Nelson felt *strongly* about something, he fought for it!

> "I knew it was
> # FOOLHARDY
> *for me to leave Fort Hare,*
> *but at the moment when*
> *I needed to compromise,*
>
> # I SIMPLY COULD
> # NOT DO SO.
> *Something inside me*
> *would not let me."*

And – just as the headmaster had threatened – Nelson was expelled.

Leaving home

When Nelson and Justice went back to the Great Place, they discovered that the chief was arranging marriages for them. The boys didn't agree with the tradition of arranged marriages, and wanted to be free to choose whomever they wanted to marry.

An ARRANGED marriage happens when the bride or groom is chosen not by the couple themselves, but by family members, like their parents. Sometimes the parents make choices for religious reasons.

Nelson and Justice **ran away** together, sharing one suitcase, and headed for the biggest city in South Africa – Johannesburg. At the time, black people weren't allowed to travel without specific documents, including a letter from their employer allowing travel between districts. The young men didn't have these documents, but they managed to get a ride from a white woman. They paid her nearly all the money they had, and had to sit in the back.

Diamonds and gold were mined in *Johannesburg*, so there were areas of great wealth. This city could give the young men new opportunities – but, as they soon discovered, Johannesburg came with its own problems.

"Johannesburg had always been depicted as

A CITY OF DREAMS,

a place where one could transform oneself from a poor peasant into a wealthy sophisticate,

A CITY OF DANGER AND OPPORTUNITY."

White people were in charge, and black people were treated poorly, as if they were second-class citizens.

The black population lived in over-crowded areas called townships. These were often built on the outskirts of towns and cities. Sometimes the houses were just made from scrap, like bits of wood that people had found. Black people found it difficult to get jobs, and often the townships had no medical facilities in case people got sick.

This unfair treatment meant that times were hard for many.

"**THE ROADS WERE UNPAVED AND DIRTY,** and filled with hungry, undernourished children scampering around half naked . . . **POOLS OF STINKING, STAGNANT WATER FULL OF MAGGOTS** collected by the side of the road."

Nelson lived in a township called **Alexandra**, where he stayed with a cousin. The cousin introduced Nelson to a black businessman named **Walter Sisula,** and Walter found Nelson a job in a law firm, working as a clerk for a white lawyer called Lazar Sidelsky.

Lazar worked for both black and white people, which was unusual when the divide between black people and white people was so great.

Nelson worked DILIGENTLY. In the daytime, he worked at the law firm, and at night he studied through a correspondence course, trying to finish the degree he'd started at Fort Hare.

DILIGENTLY:
working hard every day, doing one's best, and taking it very seriously.

After passing his exams by correspondence, Nelson decided to study law. He enrolled at **Witwatersrand University** (called "Wits").

At that time, only four universities in the whole of South Africa would let black people study. And even at Wits, Nelson still came across racism and **unfair** treatment.

Politics

Nelson made new friends at the university, both black and white. Many of them knew a lot about politics and what was happening in South Africa.

"Wits opened a new world to me, a world of ideas, and political beliefs, and debates,

A WORLD WHERE PEOPLE WERE PASSIONATE ABOUT POLITICS."

His friends agreed that black South Africans should be able to do the *same things* as white South Africans. Why should there be any difference in how they were treated? But people in the government were white, and the majority of black people were not even allowed to vote.

If they couldn't vote, how could they say anything about how they were treated? How would anything change?

"An African child
is born in
AN AFRICANS ONLY HOSPITAL,
taken home in
AN AFRICANS ONLY BUS,
lives in
AN AFRICANS ONLY AREA
and attends
AFRICANS ONLY SCHOOLS,
if he attends school
at all."

The African National Congress

The ANC was a political group started in 1912. All the members of the ANC had similar ideas about how their country should be run - they believed Africans and Europeans should have the same rights, including being able to vote.

The ANC believed in PEACEFUL COOPERATION and tried to change things to *make life fair* for black South Africans.

PEACEFUL COOPERATION: working with others to achieve a goal, without any force or violence.

Nelson wanted to be involved with the ANC. When he was twenty-six years old, he, his friend Oliver Tambo, and a few others started **the Youth League** as a new group within the ANC.

That same year, 1944, Nelson married **Evelyn Ntoko Mase**. They went on to have four children together, though Nelson's dedication to his political activities put a **strain** on their marriage.

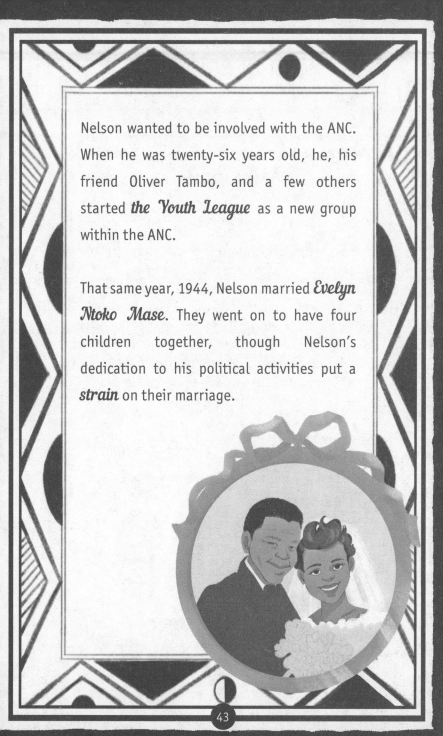

What is apartheid?

*I*n 1948, when Nelson was thirty years old, the National Party of South Africa introduced apartheid as *law*.

Even before apartheid was official, anti-African laws had been practiced for many years, since Europeans arrived (or "colonized" the land) in the seventeenth century. Life was already hard and unfair for black people. They had most of their land taken away and were prevented from getting skilled jobs. But apartheid made everything worse because black and white people were forced to live completely separately.

Rules under apartheid

No black South African could vote in elections.

Black people and white people couldn't
marry each other.

Black people were told where to live and were
moved out to places labeled "homelands."

All nonwhite people were affected by the new apartheid laws because the government had created four different racial groups.

1) White
2) Asian (from India and Pakistan)
3) Colored (mixed race)
4) Bantu (black)

The *government* put everyone into these groups, and that grouping determined where you could live, if you could go to school, where you could work, where you could travel, and where you could be treated if you became ill.

Only people classed as "white" could vote. They had the *best opportunities*, and government money was spent on making life better for them. Many black, Asian, and mixed-race people lived in *poverty*.

DID YOU KNOW?

When the National Party came to power, 75% of the people in the country were black - but 25% of people held all the power, just because they had white skin.

Signs saying "Whites Only" were put up on beaches and in restaurants. Other political groups tried to fight these laws, and the ANC asked other countries for help, but nothing changed.

Passbooks were also introduced. These books showed where black South Africans were allowed to work. A black person couldn't travel around freely unless they showed their passbook to anyone demanding to see it.

DID YOU KNOW?

The word "apartheid" means "separateness" in Afrikaans.

Protests

On May 1, 1950, a one-day **Freedom Strike** was held. Many people refused to go to work. They hoped that this resistance would start to make a difference. Nelson and his friend Walter saw **peaceful** protesters in the street. But then the police turned up and started using **guns** on the peaceful protesters.

"WE DIVED TO THE GROUND, AND REMAINED THERE *as mounted police galloped into the crowd.*"

Even though the protest had been peaceful, eighteen protesters died. They had stood up for what they believed in, but now it seemed to be *against the law* for black people to show they disagreed.

Nelson and his friends knew they could end up in prison if they protested further.

In 1951, Nelson was ELECTED National President of the Youth League of the ANC. He passionately believed in the cause he was fighting for – *freedom and fairness*. But working so much for the ANC meant that his studies suffered.

ELECTED:
chosen for government by citizens voting.

Eventually, he also qualified as a lawyer. In 1952, Nelson and Oliver Tambo set up the first black law firm. They offered low-cost or free legal advice to black people and were very busy because many black people had experienced unfair treatment.

"It was a crime to walk through a WHITES ONLY DOOR, a crime to ride a WHITES ONLY BUS, a crime to use a WHITES ONLY DRINKING FOUNTAIN, a crime to walk on a WHITES ONLY BEACH, a crime to be on the streets after 11 p.m., a crime NOT TO HAVE A PASSBOOK and a crime to have the WRONG SIGNATURE IN THAT BOOK, a crime to be UNEMPLOYED and a crime to be EMPLOYED IN THE WRONG PLACE, a crime to live in CERTAIN PLACES and a crime to have NO PLACE TO LIVE."

The ANC suggested to their members that perhaps BOYCOTTS and STRIKES might make a difference, but they should continue to protest peacefully.

STRIKE:
refusing to work because you disagree about your treatment, working conditions, or pay.

BOYCOTT:
a protest that means you stop buying from, or dealing with, a certain organization or country.

Peaceful defiance

*T*he ANC and the SAIC (South African Indian Congress) joined to create *the Defiance Campaign*.

They decided to coordinate Africans and Indians to go into the "Whites Only" areas en masse. If hundreds of black people traveled on "Whites Only" buses, and used the "Whites Only" bathrooms and waiting rooms, then the government couldn't arrest everyone at once, could they?

Nelson and his friends hoped things would change if lots of people protested and showed they were *unhappy* with the government. He knew he would get into trouble if he was caught, but this was important. He traveled around the country asking for *help and support*. He tried to inform everyone about what was happening, and explained that life would only get better if everyone worked together.

"It is what we make out of what we have,

not what we are given, that separates one person from another."

Over six months, that's exactly what happened. Over 8,000 people were arrested as a result – including Nelson! He had to go to court.

As punishment, Nelson was sentenced to nine months imprisonment with hard labor, SUSPENDED for two years. He wasn't allowed to leave Johannesburg for six months. He wasn't allowed to go to any meetings, or be seen talking to more than one person at a time, in case he was planning more protests.

The government had their eye on Nelson.

SUSPENDED SENTENCE:

the person convicted is free, but goes to prison immediately to serve their sentence – nine months, in Nelson's case – if they commit another crime within the time stated.

The Freedom Charter

*N*elson now needed to continue his work *in secret*, not letting the police or government know what was being planned.

In 1955, fifty thousand volunteers went out into townships and the countryside, handing out *leaflets* from the ANC asking people what laws *they* would make if they had the chance.

A *Freedom Charter* was created from their replies.
The charter had these headings:

- The People Shall Govern.
- All National Groups Shall Have
  Equal Rights.
- The People Shall Share In The
  Country's Wealth.
- The Land Shall Be Shared Among
  Those Who Work It.
- All Shall Be Equal Before The Law.
- All Shall Enjoy Equal Human Rights.
- There Shall Be Work And Security.
- The Doors Of Learning And Of Culture
  Shall Be Opened.
- There Shall Be Houses, Security And
  Comfort.
- There Shall Be Peace And Friendship!

Along with these statements were detailed ideas
about what the people wanted.

More different political groups came together to form a new political group called the *Congress Alliance*.

Although the members were of different ethnicities, everyone had the same goal – fair treatment, and to be able to live and work without being punished just for the color of their skin.

Because the Congress Alliance was made up of many **political groups**, it was a scarier threat to the South African government. They weren't just dealing with small **minority** groups who were easy to ignore.

The treason trial

*I*n December 1956, at the age of thirty-eight, Nelson attended a rally in disguise, but he and 155 others were arrested for *civil disobedience* – going against what the government wanted.

They were all put on trial for TREASON. Nelson had to go back and forth to court many times. They could have been sentenced to death for breaking the law, but they were eventually all declared *not guilty*.

TREASON:
the serious crime of betraying the country and trying to overthrow the government.

Because so many people were involved, the trial took four and a half years!

Nelson was still working for the ANC, trying to do what he believed was right. Protests in the country were growing, and people were getting angrier and angrier. Nelson went underground and began planning for a **national strike** (though this strike ended up being called off).

During his trial for treason, Nelson divorced Evelyn and was remarried to Nomzamo Winifred Madikizela, who was much younger than him. He and *Winnie*, as she was known, would go on to have two daughters – Zenani and Zindziswa.

The Sharpeville massacre

*I*n 1960, during an unarmed protest in Sharpeville in the Transvaal province, police shot and killed sixty-nine people. More than two hundred people were also injured.

Newspapers around the world showed images of the violence. Now, everyone knew what terrible things were happening in South Africa. The government worried they were losing **control and power**, so they made every anti-apartheid group **illegal** and banned them completely.

"The Johannesburg stock exchange plunged,

AND CAPITAL STARTED TO FLOW OUT OF THE COUNTRY.

South African whites began making plans to emigrate."

Nelson got arrested, even though he had nothing to do with the Sharpeville protests. He was sent to **prison** for five months.

*"We were given
no blankets, no food,
no mats, and no toilet paper."*

Nelson's friend Oliver Tambo escaped South Africa, moved abroad, and set up ANC offices elsewhere, eventually settling in London, England, until 1990.

When Nelson was released from prison, he decided to be *careful* about what he would do next. He *disguised* himself, traveled at night with other ANC members, and met with news reporters in secret. He told them how bad things were.

Nelson now began to think that peaceful protests might not be enough. People were still getting killed, so perhaps it was time for more *extreme* ideas. He set up another political group, separate from the ANC, called *Umkhonto we Sizwe* (Spear of the Nation).

Umkhonto we Sizwe decided they would damage property, like power lines and railroad stations. If the buildings the government cared about so much got damaged, maybe that would make an impact.

In January 1962, Nelson traveled out of South Africa without a passport – he couldn't get one because of his past arrests. He took the name **David Motsamayi** and visited other African countries, and Europe too. He told political leaders what was happening and tried to raise support for the ANC.

He returned to South Africa in July, but was **arrested** again, this time for leaving the country without a passport, as well as for encouraging people to strike.

Nelson was sent to **Pretoria Central Prison** for five years.

But he had lots of support by now. Crowds of people sang "God Bless Africa" as he was driven away.

In prison, most of the guards were white and treated black prisoners badly. Nelson was supposed to call them "boss" and wear shorts as if he were a little boy. Nelson didn't like this. He often didn't eat the food either. Nelson didn't agree with his treatment, and he **wouldn't cooperate** just to make his life easier.

But he knew his attitude would have to change, or else he was in for a miserable time.

After six months, Nelson was sent to *Robben Island*. This prison was seven miles away from land, completely cut off from the outside world. The conditions were worse than the other prison. He was only allowed one visitor and one letter every *six months*.

The Rivonia Trial

*I*n 1963 the police raided a **secret hideout** used by rebel political parties, and found papers and plans in Nelson's handwriting. This evidence proved he was involved with the Spear of the Nation violence. Although Nelson was *already* in prison, this crime was **more serious** than the one he'd been given his five-year sentence for.

Eight men, including Nelson's friend Walter and a white Jewish man, were all sentenced to **life imprisonment**. The case took six months to sort out.

Nelson defended himself in court. Here are some things he said in his three-hour speech, before he was **sent to prison for life** on June 12, 1964:

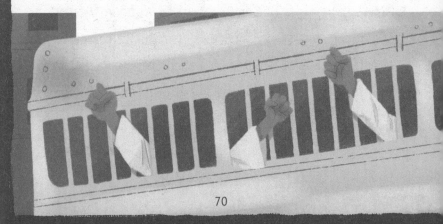

"It was only when all else had failed,
when all channels of peaceful protest had
been barred to us, that the decision was
made to embark on violent forms of
political struggle, and to form
Umkhonto we Sizwe . . .
the Government had left us no other
choice."

"I have cherished the ideal of a democratic
and free society in which
all persons live together in harmony
and with equal opportunities."

"It is an ideal which I hope to live for and
to achieve. But if needs be, it is an ideal for
which I am prepared to die."

Robben Island

*B*efore this new life sentence, Nelson had shared a large cell that had a shower and toilet, but now he was moved to a new area just for *political prisoners*. They were treated worse than any other criminal.

He had no toilet, just a bucket. Nelson's cell was a little less than six feet long – his head touched one end and his feet the other. The prisoners had no radio or newspapers. And Nelson was supposed to be there for the rest of his life!

Children weren't allowed to visit prisons, so Nelson couldn't see his children. When his wife, Winnie, visited, thick glass separated them, so they couldn't hug or kiss each other.

DID YOU KNOW?

Today, Robben Island isn't a prison, but a museum.

The prison routine

Nelson had to stay in his cell for sixteen hours a day. He had no watch or clock, so he marked the wall to show time passing. The prisoners did hard **physical labor**. Sometimes they broke up huge stones into smaller pieces, and other times they were taken to a quarry to dig out limestone with picks and shovels.

Even from inside prison, Nelson and other inmates *protested* their awful conditions. Once, when they were ordered to fill huge buckets with stones, and they had been trying their best for weeks, they went on a "go slow" strike. Although the guards threatened them, they carried on working at half the speed they had before.

Knowing that he'd be in prison for a long time, Nelson decided to **make the best** out of an awful situation. He wanted to keep his brain **active**. He told the guards that everyone should have the right to study. After many months, this was eventually allowed. Nelson and the other educated prisoners helped prisoners who couldn't **read or write**.

He exercised too, knowing that keeping fit and healthy was important. He fought hard for the few things that he could control. He wouldn't let prison life destroy him or his spirit. Nelson drew on his self-discipline and never gave up.

As the years stretched on, Nelson studied many different subjects including Afrikaans history and language. He believed if he could speak to the guards in their own language, that could only be a good thing.

"If you talk to a man
in a language
he understands,
that goes to his head.

If you talk to him
in his language,
that goes
to his heart."

He also started to write his own life story, *Long Walk to Freedom*, although he was caught in the act. As punishment, he wasn't allowed to study for *four years*.

Nelson had a small vegetable garden and grew tomatoes, onions, and chilies. But knowing exactly what was going on in the **outside world** was difficult. With no TV or newspapers, and letters restricted, he had to rely on arriving prisoners coming in with news.

He found ways, however, of passing messages to other prisoners, who were kept under less strict conditions. Then they passed the messages on to visitors, who took them into the world. Or, if a prisoner was leaving, messages were hidden in their belongings.

Nelson drew inspiration and comfort from a poem called "Invictus," by William Ernest Henley. Have you read it? There's a very famous line that reads:

"I AM THE MASTER OF MY FATE, I AM THE CAPTAIN OF MY SOUL."

Time for change

*D*uring the 1970s, a movement called BLACK CONSCIOUSNESS was gaining in popularity, particularly across the US. More people were protesting about apartheid.

BLACK CONSCIOUSNESS:

a movement that fought to overthrow apartheid. Black people from many countries began to stand together in the fight for their rights, demanding equal treatment.

In 1976, twenty thousand schoolchildren, angry at being forced to learn lessons in Afrikaans (which wasn't their language), protested in *Soweto*, Johannesburg. A few protesters threw things when the police arrived because they were so upset.

The police fought back using guns – against children! A twelve-year-old boy died. The shocking photo of him being carried in his brother's arms was shared around the world. Such a *powerful image* made people sad and angry.

The protests and fighting carried on. It is believed that more than six hundred people died.

From prison, Nelson heard about Soweto. He wrote a statement showing his support.

"*I learned that* COURAGE WAS NOT THE ABSENCE OF FEAR, *but the triumph over it. The brave man is not he who does not feel afraid,* BUT HE WHO CONQUERS THAT FEAR."

The world has had enough

The Soweto Uprising was a big turning point. The world had had enough of the fighting in South Africa. People who disagreed with what was happening started to boycott South African products. Many countries stopped doing business with South Africa, to show that they disagreed with apartheid. This damaged the economy, which made the government reconsider what it was doing.

Some countries refused to play sports with South Africa. In 1970 the International Cricket Council banned South Africa from playing cricket in competition with other countries.

Free Nelson Mandela!

*N*elson's words were **banned** in South Africa. It was illegal to show his picture. But *outside* South Africa, support for him grew and grew. He was "the face" of the apartheid fight.

In England, Oliver Tambo spoke to many different groups and started a campaign to free Nelson. In the 1980s the "Free Nelson Mandela" campaign grew.

In the UK, during the 1980s, there was a famous pop song called "Free Nelson Mandela." Later, in 1988, when Nelson was seventy years old, a huge concert was held in London with famous singers showing their support for him.

The world was watching. The South African government knew they had to do *something*.

After Nelson had been on Robben Island for eighteen years, he was moved to *Pollsmoor Prison* in Cape Town. Here, life for Nelson was nicer and more comfortable. He had a shower, a toilet, and a bed. He could watch TV and listen to the radio. There was a library.

Winnie visited, and this time no glass barriers were in the way. His grandchildren also visited for the first time.

P. W. Botha, the South African president at the time, tried to strike a deal. He promised if Nelson agreed to talk about how bad the violence was, then he would free him. But Nelson refused. He wanted freedom for *all* his people, not only himself. Although Nelson's **living conditions** were better, they weren't better for everyone. What Botha was offering wasn't fair.

Nelson carried on talking to other politicians.

After becoming ill, he was moved again, this time to a house in Victor Verster Prison. The government didn't want Nelson to die in prison – especially because the rest of the world supported him so much.

Nelson finally lived in a house, but it was still within prison walls. He was not free. But now, South Africa had a new leader – F. W. de Klerk.

De Klerk *used* to agree with apartheid, but he saw how it was tearing his country apart. He realized the system needed to *change* – it could not carry on as it had before. He released the political prisoners from Robben Island. Then he met Nelson and lifted the ban on the ANC.

"DO NOT JUDGE ME
BY MY
SUCCESSES,
judge me by
HOW MANY TIMES
I fell down and
got back up again."

Freedom at last

On February 11, 1990, at the age of seventy-one, Nelson Mandela was released from prison and finally free!

Millions of people all over the world watched Nelson and his wife walk through the prison gates – a historic moment.

"As I walked out the door toward the gate that would LEAD TO MY FREEDOM, I knew if I didn't leave my bitterness and hatred behind, I'D STILL BE IN PRISON."

In Cape Town, Nelson made his first speech as a free man:

"I STAND HERE BEFORE YOU NOT AS A PROPHET *but as a humble servant of you, the people.* **YOUR TIRELESS AND HEROIC SACRIFICES** *have made it possible for me to be here today. I therefore place the remaining years of my life* **IN YOUR HANDS."**

DID YOU KNOW?

*100,000 people were waiting in
Cape Town after Nelson was released.*

Healing a country

Nelson was out of prison, and South Africa had a **new president**. But this didn't automatically mean life would improve overnight. Years and years of fighting had **divided** the country. Lots of work had to be done to heal it.

Nelson worked for the ANC again. He traveled to fourteen different countries to express his thanks for their support. He also raised funds for the ANC.

De Klerk had changed some apartheid laws. For instance, now black people could use the same buildings as white people. They still didn't have a vote, though. He and Nelson had meetings to discuss how they could make the country a **better place**, and how things might work out between the white and black South Africans.

DID YOU KNOW?

In 1993 Nelson was jointly given the Nobel Peace Prize with de Klerk.

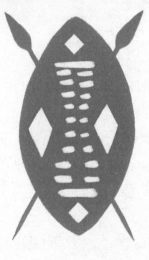

Violence was still happening regularly too. In the poorer areas, people had very different ideas about how to improve things, and even different groups of black people were *no longer united*. For example, the Zulus (Inkatha), another political party, didn't agree with the ANC – they worried that their own unique and special way of life and long traditions might disappear in the new South Africa.

Equality

*A*partheid was finally **abolished** in 1991.

Three years later, South Africa had its first election where everyone could vote, no matter what color their skin.

Nineteen different political parties campaigned for people's votes. **Nearly twenty million people voted**. News footage around the world showed people lining up to vote. Some waited for hours. It was a **momentous** occasion.

To win an election there had to be a majority – and the ANC won with 62% of the vote. Nelson Mandela became South Africa's **first black president** in 1994. He was seventy-five years old.

In his *election speech*, he said:

"We might have
our differences,
BUT WE ARE ONE PEOPLE
WITH A COMMON DESTINY
in our rich variety
OF CULTURE, RACE
AND TRADITION."

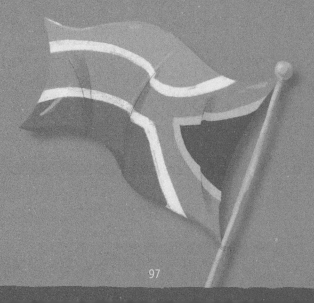

Apartheid had caused lots of damage. Nelson wanted equality for everyone, but it wasn't going to be easy. He wanted people to work together, and for no one to suffer from *discrimination*, but many black people had a bad quality of life because of all the years of apartheid, and lived in poverty. It would take more than changing some laws to make everything equal.

Nelson Mandela was president for only one term – *five years*. He made sure to include people from different races, religions, and political parties in his government. He set up schemes to try to improve things, for example, in the area of education. As president, he CAMPAIGNED for *all* South African children to have the right to an education.

CAMPAIGN: planned activities carried out to get a particular result.

When he wasn't staying in the **presidential house**, Nelson headed to the countryside, near Qunu, where he had grown up. He had a simple one-story house built, with fantastic views of the hills. The hills reminded him of his life as a young boy.

The Rugby World Cup

Some racist white South African people were unhappy that South Africa now had a black president. Nelson realized that sports could be a way for the country to unite, because sports brought people together.

In 1995, South Africa hosted the Rugby World Cup. Nelson supported South Africa's mainly white team, the Springboks, and when they won, he presented the *gold trophy* to the captain while wearing a Springboks shirt and cap. This was a clear sign to the white South Africans that Nelson was showing support and respect to them. This gesture went a long way to his becoming more accepted as their president.

There is a film about Nelson Mandela and the South African rugby team, starring Morgan Freeman as Nelson, called INVICTUS.

Nearly twenty-five years later, in 2019, South Africans of all skin colors celebrated together when a mixed-race Springboks team, headed by a black captain, took home the Rugby World Cup.

Nelson retired at age eighty-one, and went to live full-time in Qunu. He wanted to spend time with his family.

Even after retirement, however, he raised awareness of the issues in South Africa. At the Live 8 concert held in 2005, his speech included these words:

"Sometimes it falls upon
a generation to be great.
You be that great generation.
Let your greatness blossom.
Of course the task
will not be easy.
But not to do this would be a
crime against humanity,
against which I ask
all humanity now
to rise up."

JULY

SUNDAY	MONDAY	TUESDAY	WEDNESDAY	THURSDAY	FRIDAY	SATURDAY
			1	2	3	4
5	6	7	8	9	10	11
12	13	14	15	16	17	18 *67 minutes of help*
19	20	21	22	23	24	25
26	27	28	29	30	31	

July 18 is Nelson Mandela Day. This day of international celebration was created by the United Nations (UN), an organization that promotes teamwork between different countries. People are asked to spend sixty-seven minutes helping others (for the sixty-seven years Mandela served his country).

Mandela and family

*B*alancing being a father to his children with being a "father" to his country was a struggle for Nelson Mandela. At times, especially when they were young, his children didn't understand why their father wasn't around for them.

Nelson was married three times. Sometimes couples grow apart, especially if they're living under such **challenging** conditions. He divorced his first wife, Evelyn, partly because she wasn't as politically active as he was. She didn't agree with how Nelson spent his time. He divorced his second wife, Winnie, because, although she *was* politically active and supported him while he was in prison, she had been involved in some **extreme** political acts. They often disagreed on how best to fight for what they believed in.

On his eightieth birthday, in 1998, Nelson married Graça Machel, a politician and humanitarian.

Nelson died on December 5, 2013, at the age of 95. He was with his family and had been suffering from a respiratory infection.

Nelson had six children altogether – four daughters and two sons – as well as *seventeen grandchildren*.

Sadly, Nelson outlived three of his children.

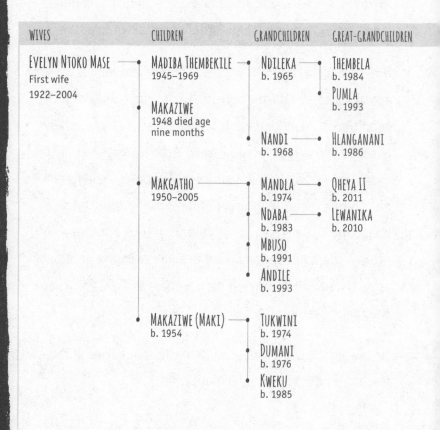

WIVES	CHILDREN	GRANDCHILDREN	GREAT-GRANDCHILDREN
EVELYN NTOKO MASE First wife 1922–2004	MADIBA THEMBEKILE 1945–1969	NDILEKA b. 1965	THEMBELA b. 1984 PUMLA b. 1993
	MAKAZIWE 1948 died age nine months	NANDI b. 1968	HLANGANANI b. 1986
	MAKGATHO 1950–2005	MANDLA b. 1974	QHEYA II b. 2011
		NDABA b. 1983	LEWANIKA b. 2010
		MBUSO b. 1991	
		ANDILE b. 1993	
	MAKAZIWE (MAKI) b. 1954	TUKWINI b. 1974	
		DUMANI b. 1976	
		KWEKU b. 1985	

In 1948 Nelson's daughter Makaziwe passed away in a hospital at only nine months old; in 1969 his elder son Madiba Thembekile died in a car accident, and in 2005 his other son, Makgatho, passed away after a hard battle with AIDS.

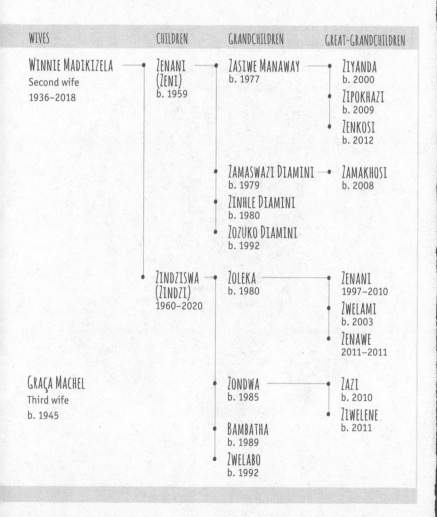

WIVES	CHILDREN	GRANDCHILDREN	GREAT-GRANDCHILDREN
WINNIE MADIKIZELA Second wife 1936–2018	ZENANI (ZENI) b. 1959	ZASIWE MANAWAY b. 1977	ZIYANDA b. 2000
			ZIPOKHAZI b. 2009
			ZENKOSI b. 2012
		ZAMASWAZI DIAMINI b. 1979	ZAMAKHOSI b. 2008
		ZINHLE DIAMINI b. 1980	
		ZOZUKO DIAMINI b. 1992	
	ZINDZISWA (ZINDZI) 1960–2020	ZOLEKA b. 1980	ZENANI 1997–2010
			ZWELAMI b. 2003
			ZENAWE 2011–2011
GRAÇA MACHEL Third wife b. 1945		ZONDWA b. 1985	ZAZI b. 2010
			ZIWELENE b. 2011
		BAMBATHA b. 1989	
		ZWELABO b. 1992	

Nelson Mandela will be remembered as a man who believed in **kindness** and **equality**. He left behind a *legacy* of unity and peace, and was one of the greatest leaders the world has ever seen.

"What counts in life is not the mere fact THAT WE HAVE LIVED. It is what DIFFERENCE we have made to the LIVES OF OTHERS that will determine the SIGNIFICANCE OF THE LIFE WE LEAD."

TIMELINE

July 18, 1918
Nelson (Rolihlahla) is born.

1926
Nelson moves to Qunu.

1930
His father dies and Nelson moves to the Great Place.

1939
Nelson attends Fort Hare University.

1951

Nelson qualifies as a lawyer.

1948

The National Party wins the election.
Apartheid becomes law.

1944

Cofounds the ANC Youth League.
Marries Evelyn Mase.

1942

Studies law at
Witwatersrand and
joins the ANC.

1941

Starts working as a clerk at a
law office in Johannesburg.

1952

Nelson and Oliver Tambo set up the first black law firm in Johannesburg.

Passbook laws introduced.

1955

Joins the Congress Alliance and consults on the Freedom Charter. Separates from Evelyn.

1956

Nelson and 155 others arrested for treason.

1958

Divorces Evelyn. Marries Winnie.

1960

Sharpeville massacre, at which sixty-nine people die. ANC banned.

1982

Nelson is moved to
Pollsmoor Prison.

1976

Soweto massacre,
over 200 people dead.

1964

People from the Rivonia
Trial all sentenced to life
imprisonment.

Arrives on Robben Island
in June 1964.

1961

Nelson forms Umkhonto
we Sizwe and goes
underground.

1984

Nelson's first contact visit with Winnie in over twenty-one years.

1988

Nelson is ill with tuberculosis and moves to Victor Verster prison.

1990

Nelson is released from prison after twenty-seven years.

1991

Apartheid abolished.

1992

Nelson separates from Winnie.

2013

Nelson dies on December 5, at age ninety-five.

1998

Nelson's eightieth birthday. He marries Graça Machel.

1994

Mandela becomes the first black president of South Africa.

1993

Mandela and de Klerk jointly awarded the Nobel Peace Prize.

Some things to think about

Sadly, some people still face discrimination today. People can be treated poorly because of their race, religion, gender, or sexuality.

Do you think this is right? What do you think you could do to help people get along?

Do your school or teachers already know about Mandela Day?

Nelson Mandela, Martin Luther King Jr., Rosa Parks, and Mahatma Gandhi were individuals who witnessed people being treated unfairly. They decided to take a stand and to do something about it. You do not have to accept unfair treatment. Can you think of anyone else who has stood up for what they believe?

What do you think we can do if we see unfair treatment?

We can speak up. That's a choice Nelson made repeatedly. He witnessed unfairness and wanted to change things, even though he was punished for it. Because of his dignity and determination, his empathy and acceptance of other people, he managed to lead a country to freedom. Even if, as he says in his life story, it was a "long walk."

Why do you think Nelson believed education to be so important?

Nelson knew that knowledge was invaluable, and with proper education people have the ability to change their circumstances in life. If everyone is given the same knowledge about life, that brings us one step closer to equality. And, as Nelson once said, with education "a child of farmworkers can become the president of a great nation" – like Nelson himself!

Why do you think Nelson was so influential in the fight for equality?

Nelson proved that if you feel passionately about a cause you should not give up. What can you learn from his extraordinary life that you can apply to your own life?

Index

Quote Sources

Direct quotes throughout are taken from *Long Walk to Freedom* by Nelson Mandela (Abacus, October 1995), except the below:

Page 109: Address by Nelson Mandela during the 90th birthday celebration of Mr. Walter Sisulu, 18 May 2002: http://www.mandela.gov.za/mandela_speeches/2002/020518_sisulu.htm

Have you read about all of these extraordinary people?

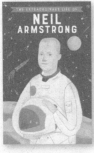